ALBERT PUJOLS
Baseball Superstar

BY JOANNE MATTERN

CAPSTONE PRESS
a capstone imprint

Sports Illustrated KIDS Superstar Athletes is published by Capstone Press,
151 Good Counsel Drive, P.O. Box 669, Mankato, Minnesota 56002.
www.capstonepub.com

Books published by Capstone Press are manufactured with paper
containing at least 10 percent post-consumer waste.

Library of Congress Cataloging-in-Publication Data
Mattern, Joanne, 1963–
 Albert Pujols : baseball superstar / by Joanne Mattern.
  p. cm.—(Sports Illustrated kids : superstar athletes)
 Includes bibliographical references and index.
 Summary: "Presents the athletic biography of Albert Pujols, including his career as a high school,
college, and professional baseball player"—Provided by publisher.
 ISBN 978-1-4296-6561-2 (library binding)
 ISBN 978-1-4296-7301-3 (paperback)
 1. Pujols, Albert, 1980– —Juvenile literature. 2. Baseball players—Dominican Republic—
Biography—Juvenile literature. 3. Baseball players—United States—Biography—Juvenile
literature. 4. St. Louis Cardinals (Baseball team)—Juvenile literature. I. Title.
 GV865.P85M382 2012
 796.357092—dc22[B]   2011001022

Editorial Credits
Christopher L. Harbo, editor; Ted Williams, designer; Eric Gohl, media researcher;
    Eric Manske, production specialist

Photo Credits
Courtesy of Just Minors, 10
Getty Images Inc./Diamond Images, 13; Robert Nickelsberg, 9
Sports Illustrated/Al Tielemans, 21, 22 (bottom); Chuck Solomon, 15; David E. Klutho, cover (all),
    2–3, 5, 7, 16, 18, 23, 24; Heinz Kluetmeier, 6; John Biever, 22 (top); John W. McDonough, 17, 22
    (middle); Robert Beck, 1

Design Elements
Shutterstock/chudo-yudo, designerpix, Fassver Anna, Fazakas Mihaly

Direct Quotations
Page 11 quoted on *Baseball Almanac*, http://www.baseball-almanac.com
Pages 14, 19 quoted on *Albert Pujols Club*, http://www.albertpujolsclub.com

Printed in the United States of America in North Mankato, Minnesota.
032011   006110CGF11

TABLE OF CONTENTS

CHAPTER 1

APRIL FIREWORKS

On April 29, 2006, Albert Pujols was chasing a record. His St. Louis Cardinals and the Washington Nationals were locked in a 1-1 tie. In the bottom of the eighth inning, Pujols stepped up to bat. He quickly got ahead in the pitch count with two balls and one strike.

Pujols swung hard at the fourth pitch. Crack! The ball leaped off his bat. Pujols' 14th home run of the season sailed into the rightfield **bullpen**.

bullpen—a place where pitchers warm up before pitching in a game

Pujols became the first player ever to hit 14 home runs during April. It was a good start to a great season. By the end of the season, he had 49 home runs and a World Series ring.

CHAPTER 2

MOVE TO AMERICA

Albert Pujols was born January 16, 1980, in the Dominican Republic. Pujols lived in Santo Domingo. He grew up playing baseball. When he was 16, he moved to the United States with his father. They settled in Missouri. Pujols played baseball at Fort Osage High School. His **batting average** rose above .500 in his first season.

batting average—a measure of how often a batter gets a hit

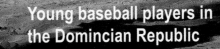

Young baseball players in the Domincian Republic

DOMINICAN BASEBALL

Baseball is very popular in the Dominican Republic. Almost every boy plays baseball. Major league teams send scouts to the Dominican Republic to find great players. More than 500 Dominicans have played in the major leagues.

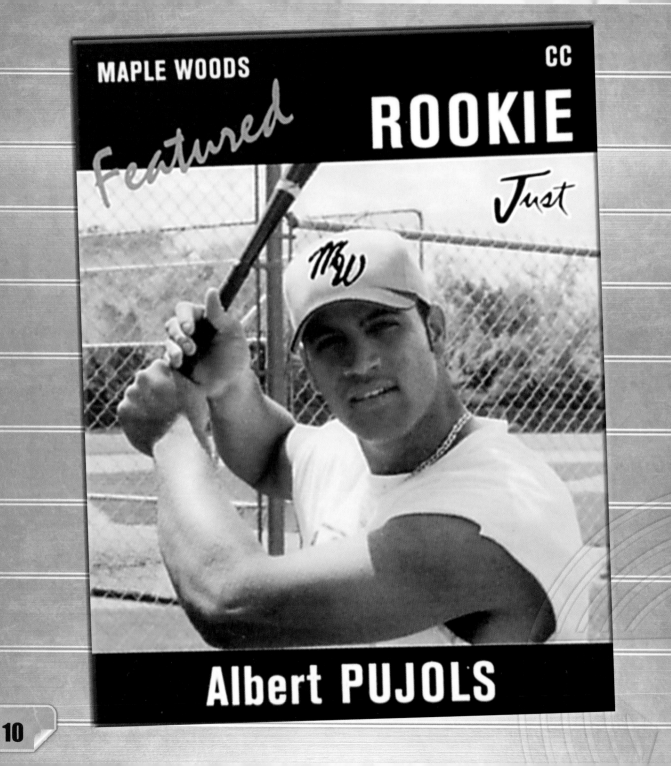

MAPLE WOODS   CC

Featured ROOKIE

Just

Albert PUJOLS

After high school, Pujols went to Maple Woods Community College. He was a star right away. Pujols had a .461 batting average his first year. He hit 22 home runs and had 80 runs batted in (RBIs). After just one year, Pujols entered the Major League Baseball (MLB) **draft**.

draft—the process of choosing a person to join a sports team

"You know if you work hard, your hard work is going to pay off someday." —Albert Pujols

CHAPTER 3

CARDINAL STAR

In June 1999, the St. Louis Cardinals drafted Pujols in the 13th round. In September he joined a Cardinals' **minor league** team. In 2000 Pujols' batting average climbed to .324. He also hit 17 home runs. He was named the minor league Most Valuable Player (MVP).

minor league—a league of teams where players improve their playing skills before joining a major league team

Pujols joined the Cardinals as an infielder in 2001. He wasted no time wowing fans. In each of his first two seasons, he had more than 30 home runs and 100 RBIs. In 2003 Pujols brought even more power to the plate. He racked up 212 hits and smashed 43 home runs. He was the National League batting champion with a .359 average.

"Sometimes you're going to get hits. Sometimes you're going to make outs. That's the way this game is. You're not going to be perfect every time." —Albert Pujols

Pujols' playing skills improved over the next few seasons. He hit 46 home runs in 2004. In 2005 he had a .330 batting average and 117 RBIs. He was also named the National League MVP.

In 2006 Pujols shined in the field too. He won the Gold Glove Award at first base. He also helped the Cardinals win the World Series.

AMAZING RECORD

In 2010, Pujols hit more than 30 home runs for the 10th straight season in a row. No other player has ever achieved this record.

Pujols continued to put up great numbers in 2008 and 2009. In 2008 he had a .357 batting average and 37 home runs. In 2009 he hit 47 homers. He repeated as the National League MVP in both seasons. In 2010 he won another Gold Glove Award at first base.

"There is no pressure. I just concentrate and do the best I can. I try to do my best every day and help the team win any way I can." —Albert Pujols

CHAPTER 4

POWERFUL PLAYMAKER

Albert Pujols is one of baseball's most popular players. He hits with power and adds a great glove to the infield. Fans know that when Pujols plays, the game will be exciting. They expect him to knock out home runs and make diving plays at first base. Game after game, Pujols delivers.

TIMELINE

1980—Albert Pujols is born January 16 in the Dominican Republic.

1996—Pujols moves to Independence, Missouri; he plays baseball for Fort Osage High School.

1999—Pujols attends Maple Woods Community College; he is drafted by the St. Louis Cardinals.

2001—Pujols is named the National League's Rookie of the Year; he is also named to the National League's All-Star Team.

2005—Pujols wins the National League's Most Valuable Player award.

2006—Pujols helps the Cardinals win the World Series; he also wins his first Gold Glove award.

2010—Pujols becomes the first player to hit at least 30 home runs in 10 straight seasons.

GLOSSARY

batting average (BAT-ing AV-uh-rij)—a measure of how often a batter gets a hit

bullpen (BUL-pen)—a place where pitchers warm up before pitching in a game

draft (DRAFT)—the process of choosing a person to join a sports team

minor league (MYE-nur LEEG)—a league of teams where players improve their playing skills before joining a major league team

scout (SKOUT)—someone sent to watch and assess players and teams

READ MORE

Edwards, Ethan. *Meet Albert Pujols: Baseball's Power Hitter.* All-Star Players. New York: Powerkids Press, 2009.

Mattern, Joanne. *Albert Pujols.* A Robbie Reader. Hockessin, Del.: Mitchell Lane Publishers, 2008.

INTERNET SITES

FactHound offers a safe, fun way to find Internet sites related to this book. All of the sites on FactHound have been researched by our staff.

Here's all you do:

Visit *www.facthound.com*

Type in this code: 9781429665612

 Check out projects, games and lots more at
www.capstonekids.com

INDEX